Student Interactive

myView®
L I T E R A C Y

1

SAVVAS
LEARNING COMPANY

Julie Coiro, Ph.D.

Jim Cummins, Ph.D.

Pat Cunningham, Ph.D.

Elfrieda Hiebert, Ph.D.

Pamela Mason, Ed.D.

Ernest Morrell, Ph.D.

P. David Pearson, Ph.D.

Frank Serafini, Ph.D.

Alfred Tatum, Ph.D.

Sharon Vaughn, Ph.D.

Judy Wallis, Ed.D.

Lee Wright, Ed.D.

UNIT 2
CONTENTS

I Spy

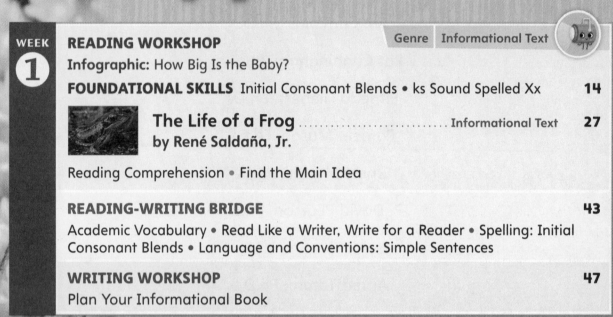

I Spy

Essential Question

How do living things grow and change?

▶ **Watch**

"Who's Been There?" See what you can learn about animal tracks.

TURN and TALK What did you learn about animal tracks?

SAVVAS **realize**™
Go ONLINE for all lessons.

▶ VIDEO

◀ AUDIO

🎮 GAME

✏ ANNOTATE

📖 BOOK

🔍 RESEARCH

Spotlight on Informational Text

Reading-Writing Bridge

- Academic Vocabulary
- Read Like a Writer, Write for a Reader
- Spelling • Language and Conventions

Writing Workshop

- Plan Your Informational Book   **Informational Book**
- Simple Graphics • Introduction and Conclusion
- Edit for Complete Sentences with Subject-Verb Agreement
- Publish and Celebrate

Project-Based Inquiry

- Inquire • Research • Collaborate

Read Together

Independent Reading

In this unit, you will read books with your teacher. You will read informational text, poetry, and drama. You will also read books on your own.

Choose a book you will enjoy reading.

I want to read:

What is your purpose, or reason, for reading?

I want to:

- Learn facts about _____
- Read a story for fun
- Read something new to me

My Reading Log

Date	Book	Pages Read	Minutes Read	My Ratings
				☺ ☐ ☹
				☺ ☐ ☹
				☺ ☐ ☹
				☺ ☐ ☹
				☺ ☐ ☹

You may wish to use a Reader's Notebook to record and respond to your reading.

Unit Goals

In this unit, you will

- read informational texts
- write an informational book
- learn about plants and animals

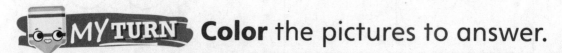 **MY TURN** **Color** the pictures to answer.

I can read informational text.	👍	👎
I can make and use words to read and write informational text.	👍	👎
I can write informational text.	👍	👎
I understand how living things grow and change.	👍	👎

Final Sounds

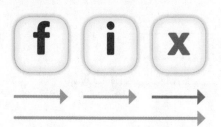 **SEE and SAY** Sometimes you hear the **ks** sound at the end of a word. Say each sound as you name each picture. Then say the name of each picture again.

ks Sound Spelled x

The letter **x** can make the **ks** sound you hear in **fox**.

MY TURN Read these words.

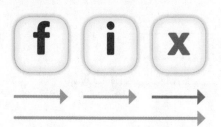
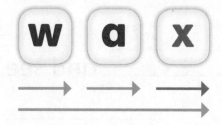

My Words to Know

Some words you must remember and practice.

MY TURN Read these words.

my	saw	help	come	little

Handwriting Always print words legibly, or clearly. Leave spaces between words.

MY TURN Finish the sentences. Print the words clearly. Leave spaces between the words.

1. Here is a _little_ fox.

2. The fox _____ me.

3. _____ and see _____ fox.

4. Mom will _____ the fox.

ks Sound Spelled x

TURN and TALK Read these words with a partner. Think about the sound **x** makes when you read the words.

fix	mix	six
ax	fax	Max
ox	box	fox
tax	sax	wax

MY TURN Write **x** to finish the words.

1. ___Fi_____ the flag.

2. Put it in the ___bo_____ .

TURN and TALK Now read the sentences.

Read
Together

ks Sound Spelled x

MY TURN Add **x** to make words. Read each word. Then draw a line from each word to its picture.

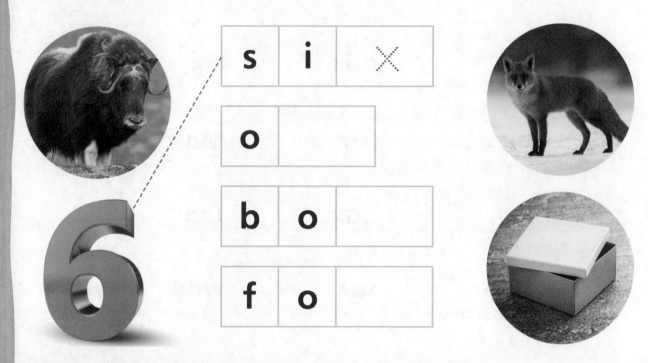

s	i	x

o		

b	o	

f	o	

MY TURN Write a sentence that includes a word with **x**.

_____

_____

_____

_____

Big Fox, Little Fox

Rex is a little fox.

His mom is a big fox.

Rex saw a crab.

The crab is on my grass.

AUDIO

Audio with Highlighting

ANNOTATE

Read the story. Highlight the six words
with the **ks** sound spelled **x.**

Snap! Snap!

Rex can not fix it.

Underline the words with initial consonant blends.

The big fox will come.

The big fox will help the little fox.

Plop!

<u>Underline</u> the word with the initial consonant blend.

I can read informational text.

SPOTLIGHT ON GENRE

Informational Text

An informational text tells about a real person, place, or thing. It has a main idea, or central, idea.

Title ──• **From Egg to Butterfly**

Main Idea ──• A butterfly goes through four stages. First, it is an

Supporting Details ──• egg. Next, it is a caterpillar. Then it builds a chrysalis. Finally, it is a butterfly.

TURN *and* **TALK** Talk about the main idea of "From Egg to Butterfly."

Informational Text
Anchor Chart

Title
names the topic

Main Idea
what the text is
mostly about

Detail Detail

Detail

Detail

Details
tell more about
the main idea

The Life of a Frog

Preview Vocabulary

You will read these words in *The Life of a Frog*.

eggs	frog	gills	tadpole

Read

Read to learn about frogs.

Look at the photos to help you understand the text.

Ask yourself questions to help you learn information.

Talk about the text with a partner.

Meet the Author

René Saldaña, Jr., is a teacher. He writes books for children. When he was a boy, his nickname was Froggy.

Find Important Details

Supporting evidence, or details, is the most important pieces of information about a main idea.

MY TURN Draw an important detail that supports the main idea. Look back at the text.

Reflect and Share

Talk About It

You read about how tadpoles grow and change into frogs. What do you know about how other animals grow and change?

Share Information and Ideas

When talking with others, it is important to:

- Share your ideas.

- Listen to others as they share their ideas.

Use the words on the note to help you share ideas and listen to others.

I know that . . .
I think that . . .

Now share your ideas.

Weekly Question

How do animals grow and change?

I can make and use words to read and write informational text.

My Learning Goal

Academic Vocabulary

Related words are connected in some way.

MY TURN Read the words by each circle. Write the related word from the box in the circle.

notice	nature	reason	pattern

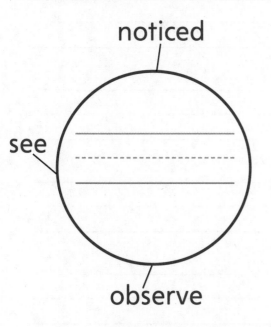

noticed

see

observe

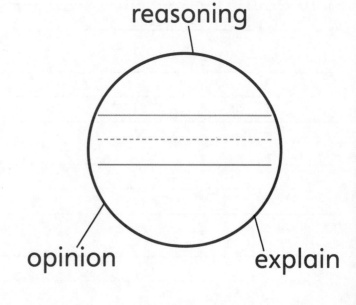

reasoning

opinion   explain

43

Read Like a Writer, Write for a Reader

Authors choose words carefully. Interesting words can help a reader visualize the meaning of the text.

It has a wiggly tail to help it swim.

The author uses this word to help readers visualize how the tail moves.

MY TURN Write sentences with interesting words that tell about a frog. The words should help you visualize the animal.

_____

_____

_____

_____

_____

_____

Read Together

Spell Words with Consonant Blends

Consonant blends are spelled with two different consonants that together make a blended sound.

 **MY TURN** Spell and sort the words.

Spelling Words

step	trip	stem	snap
snug	stop	snip	trap

tr-

trip

sn-

st-

My Words to Know

come	little

Read Together

Simple Sentences

A **sentence** tells a complete idea.
It has a **subject**, or whom
the sentence is about.
It has a **predicate** that tells what the subject
is or does. A sentence begins with a capital
letter and ends with a punctuation mark.

Be sure to add **-s** to a verb to tell what one
subject does now. When you have two or
more subjects, do not add **-s** to a verb.

The tadpole **swims.** (Add **-s**.)
The frogs **hop.** (Do not add **-s**.)

 **MY TURN** Edit the sentences.

1. Sam play at the pond

_____

2. frog legs grows longer.

_____

I can write informational text.

Informational Book

Informational books have:

- a title
- a main idea
- supporting details about the main idea

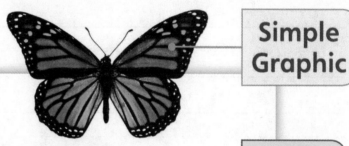

Simple Graphic

From Egg to Butterfly

Title

A butterfly goes through four stages. First, it is an egg. Next, it is a caterpillar. Then it builds a chrysalis. Finally, it is a butterfly.

Main Idea

Supporting Details

Topic and Main Idea

A **topic** is what an author writes about. Authors choose a topic they know a lot about.

MY TURN What topics do you know a lot about? Make a list of topics.

_____

- -

_____

_____

- -

_____

_____

- -

_____

The **main idea** is the most important information about the topic. Authors write main ideas after they choose a topic.

MY TURN Circle one of your topics. Write your main idea.

_____

- -

_____

_____

- -

_____

Plan Your Informational Book

MY TURN Plan your book by brainstorming and writing ideas.

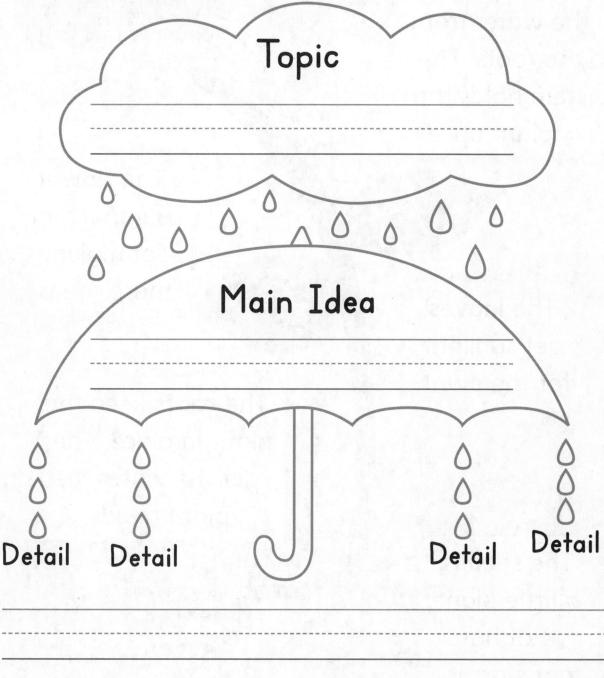

Topic

Main Idea

Detail Detail Detail Detail

Parts of a Plant

The **stem** gets the water from the roots. The stem holds the plant up.

The **flower** is important for making more seeds.

The **leaves** get sunlight for the plant.

The **roots** keep the plant in place. They get the water the plant needs.

The **seed** is a little plant that has not started to grow.

How do plants grow and change?

MY TURN Match the picture to its name.

roots

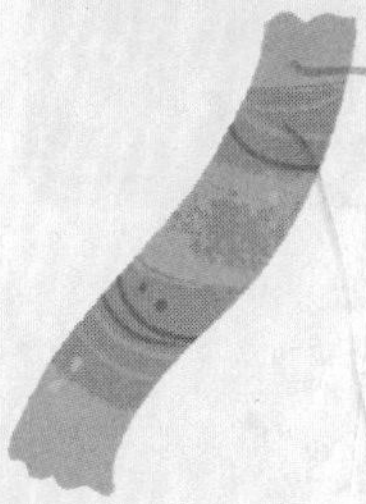

seed

leaves

flower

stem

Rhyming Words

SEE and SAY Rhyming words have the same middle and ending sounds. Say the name of each picture. Produce, or say, other words that rhyme with the picture names.

k Sound Spelled ck

The letters **ck** together make the **k** sound in **sock.**

MY TURN Read these words.

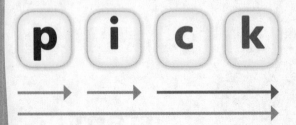 

k Sound Spelled ck

TURN and TALK Read these words with a partner.

tack	**sack**	**pack**
neck	**deck**	**peck**
kick	**tick**	**lick**
sock	**lock**	**rock**

MY TURN Write **ck** to finish the words.

1. _Pick_ the best rock.

2. Put it _ba____ in the sack.

TURN and TALK Now read the sentences.

k Sound Spelled ck

 **MY TURN** Say each picture name. Write the word that names each picture.

The final **k** sound can be spelled **ck**.

sock

_____

_____

_____

 **MY TURN** Write a sentence about a duck.

The duck _____

_____

_____

s Sound and z Sound Spelled s

TURN and TALK Read these words.

is	**his**	**has**

laps	**hats**	**racks**

MY TURN Say each picture name. Write **s** to finish the word. Read each word.

cats   can

bug   map

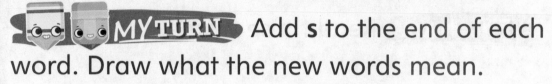

s Sound and z Sound Spelled s

 MY TURN Add **s** to the end of each word. Draw what the new words mean.

cat

bed

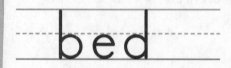 MY TURN Write a sentence about one of your pictures.

The Stems

Jack has plans for the stems.

His mom can help.

She can pick up the sack.

AUDIO

Audio with Highlighting

ANNOTATE

Read the story. Highlight the five words with the **z** sound spelled **s**.

What is in the sack?

It can help the stems get big.

They take the pots to the back.

Highlight the two words with the **k** sound spelled **ck.**

They walk by the <u>pots</u>.

Jack will jump. He is glad.

Look! The big stems have little buds.

<u>Underline</u> the three words that mean more than one.

My Learning Goal

I can read informational text.

SPOTLIGHT ON GENRE

Informational Text

Informational texts have an organizational pattern, or the way the information is organized. A text can be in chronological order, or in a sequence. A text can tell facts about a topic.

Set a Purpose The purpose, or reason, for reading informational text can be to learn about a topic.

TURN and TALK Think about an informational text you have read. Talk with a partner about your purpose for reading that text.

Read Together

Informational Text Anchor Chart

How informational text can be organized:

Sequence

description

The Life Cycle of a Sunflower

Preview Vocabulary

You will read these words in *The Life Cycle of a Sunflower.*

buds	soil	stems	leaves

Read

Read for the purpose you set.

Look at headings to help plan your reading.

Ask questions about the facts.

Talk about what you found most interesting.

Meet *the* Author

Linda Tagliaferro likes to write books that help children understand nature around them. In these pages from *The Life Cycle of a Sunflower*, notice the order of events.

Genre   Informational Text

AUDIO

Audio with
Highlighting

ANNOTATE

The Life Cycle of a Sunflower

by Linda Tagliaferro

Sunflower Seeds

How do sunflowers grow?

Sunflowers grow from the seeds of the sunflower plant.

Sunflower seeds need sunlight, soil, water, and warmth.

Then they sprout.

CLOSE READ

<u>Underline</u> the words that tell what happens after sunflower seeds get what they need.

Growing

Stems peek out on top of the soil.

Small leaves grow on the stems.

Stems fill with more leaves and branches.

Flower buds form on the branches.

Then the buds open.

CLOSE READ

<u>Underline</u> the details that describe what happens after sunflower seeds sprout.

Sunflowers!

Sunflowers bloom.

They move to face the sun.

Seeds form inside the flowers.

In fall, sunflowers bend and their <u>seeds scatter.</u>

CLOSE READ

Highlight the words that help you figure out what happens to the sunflower seeds.

Starting Over

Next year, new sunflowers grow.

The life cycle continues.

<u>Underline</u> the word that helps you figure out what **cycle** means.

How Sunflowers Grow

Glossary

branch—the part of the plant or tree that grows out of the main stem like an arm

life cycle—the stages in the life of a plant that include sprouting, reproducing, and dying

scatter—to be thrown or to fall over a wide area

seed—the part of a flowering plant that can grow into a new plant

soil—the dirt where plants grow; most plants get their food and water from the soil

sprout—to grow, appear, or develop quickly

stem—the long main part of a plant that makes leaves

Develop Vocabulary

MY TURN Read the word in each box. Then draw a picture that shows what each word means.

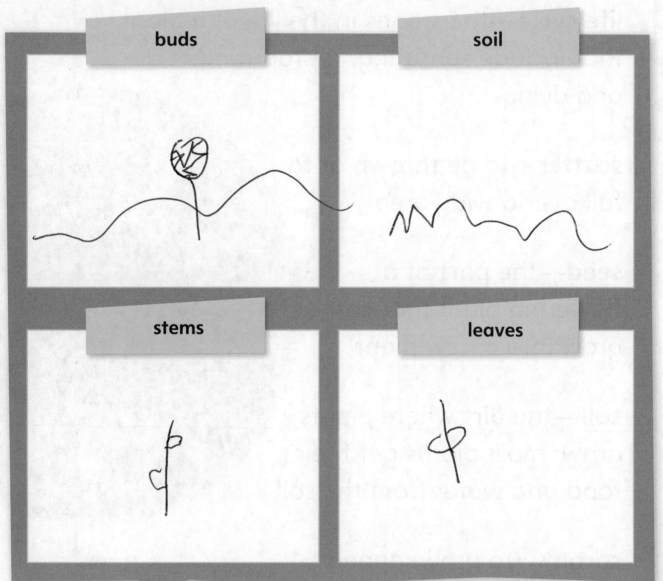

| buds | soil |
| stems | leaves |

TURN and TALK Talk about what each vocabulary word means.

Check for Understanding

MY TURN Write the answers to the questions. You can look back at the text.

1. How does the title help you know the text is informational text?

_____

_____

_____

_____

2. Why does the author use a glossary?

_____

_____

_____

_____

3. What would happen if sunflower seeds did not get what they need? Use text evidence.

_____

_____

_____

_____

Find Text Structure

An informational text can organize facts in chronological order, or in a sequence. The facts are in the order they happen in time.

MY TURN Draw what is missing in the life cycle of a sunflower. Look back at the text.

MY TURN Circle the text structure of the text.

chronological order **description**

Make Inferences

Readers use text evidence to make inferences. They use what they know and what they read to figure out something about the text.

 **MY TURN** Write an inference about *The Life Cycle of a Sunflower*. Look back at the text.

What I Read	What I Already Know

My Inference

Reflect and Share

Talk About It

You read about how sunflowers grow. What other living things have you read about that grow and change? How are they different from sunflowers?

Ask and Answer Questions

When talking with others, it is important to:

- Ask questions when you do not understand something.

- Answer questions in complete sentences.

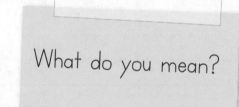

What do you mean?

Use the words on the note to help you.

Now share your ideas.

Weekly Question

How do plants grow and change?

My Learning Goal

I can make and use words to read and write informational text.

Academic Vocabulary

Synonyms are words that have similar meanings.

MY TURN Read each pair of sentences. Highlight the synonym for the underlined word.

1. I did not <u>see</u> the bug.

   I did not notice it.

2. The flowers make a <u>design</u>.

   I can see a simple pattern.

3. Please keep the <u>outdoors</u> clean.

   Nature should stay beautiful.

Read Like a Writer, Write for a Reader

Authors use sequence words to tell readers the order in which events happen. **First**, **next**, **then**, and **last** are sequence words.

Flower buds form on the branches. Then the buds open.

◄··········· The author uses this word to tell readers that the buds open after they form on the branches.

MY TURN Write about the events in your day. Use words that name sequences to tell the order.

Spell Words with ck

A closed syllable word ends with a consonant sound.

 **MY TURN** Sort and spell words that end in **ck**.

Spelling Words			
sack	tack	luck	stack
sick	back	black	stuck

-ack

sack

_____

_____

_____

-uck

_____

_____

My Words to Know

walk   what

_____

_____

-ick

_____

Declarative Sentences

A **declarative sentence** is a telling sentence. It makes a statement. It begins with a capital letter and ends with a period.

The grass is green. (tells about grass)

Be sure to use a period at the end of a declarative sentence.

MY TURN Edit the punctuation marks at the ends of these declarative sentences.

1. The plant is green!

----

2. It will grow tall?

I can write informational text.   My Learning Goal

Main Idea

An informational book has a **main idea.** The main idea tells what the book is mostly about. Authors use the main idea to focus their writing.

 **MY TURN** Read the passage. Write a main idea for the passage.

First, dig a small hole. Next, put the seed in the hole. Then, cover the seed with dirt. Last, water the seed.

_____

- - - - - - - - - - - - - - - - - - -

_____

- - - - - - - - - - - - - - - - - - -

_____

MY TURN Compose a main idea for your informational book.

Facts and Details

An informational book has facts and details. A **fact** is a piece of information that is known to be true. A **detail** is a small piece of information.

Authors use facts and details to develop a main idea. They make sure details are specific, or exact. They make sure details are relevant, or about the main idea.

MY TURN Write a fact and detail about the main idea.
Main Idea: Plants grow and change.

_____

_____

_____

_____

MY TURN Develop facts with specific and relevant details for your informational book.

Simple Graphics

Simple graphics add details to a text. They show information in a visual way. Photographs, illustrations, charts, diagrams, and maps are types of simple graphics.

MY TURN Draw a simple graphic that supports the text.

Pets

Having a pet can be fun, but it is a lot of work! You need to feed your pet, clean your pet, and play with your pet.

MY TURN Include simple graphics as you write your informational book.

Baby Animal Names

Baby animals and their parents can have different names.

Baby Animal

kitten

duckling

tadpole

Parent

duck

frog

cat

How are baby animals different from their parents?

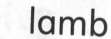 **MY TURN** Match each baby animal to its parent.

fawn

lamb

sheep

deer

Final Sounds

 **SEE and SAY** Sometimes you hear two sounds at the end of a word. Say each sound as you name each picture. Blend the sounds together to say the word again.

Final Consonant Blends

Two consonants at the end of a word that are blended together are called **final consonant blends,** like the **lk** in **milk.**

MY TURN Find two words in the classroom with final consonant blends. Write the words on the lines.

_____

_____

_____

_____

Final Consonant Blends

TURN and TALK Decode these words with a partner.

best	**land**	**help**

ask	**left**	**went**

MY TURN Read each word. <u>Underline</u> the final consonant blend. Draw a picture to show each word.

ne<u>st</u>	belt
gift	stamp

Read Together

Final Consonant Blends

 **MY TURN** Write **st**, **ft**, or **nt** to finish the words. Then read the sentences.

1. The fox is on the ___ hunt ___.

2. He can run ___ fa___.

3. What is to his ___ le___ ?

Listen for the last two sounds that are blended together.

 **MY TURN** Write another sentence about the fox. Use words with final consonant blends.

_____

_____

_____

_____

Add Sounds

SEE and SAY Say the verb that describes the action in each picture. Then add the **s** sound to the end of each verb. Say the new verbs.

Inflectional Ending -s

Adding **-s** to a verb changes its meaning. It shows that one person, animal, or thing does the action now.

MY TURN Read the sentences. <u>Underline</u> the verbs with the ending **-s**. Tell their meanings.

Jim <u>helps</u> his mom.

He packs up his bag.

Jim grabs the sack.

My Words to Know

Some words you must remember and practice.

MY TURN Read the words.

use	blue	from	this	think

MY TURN Use words from the box to complete the sentences.

Handwriting Print the words clearly.

1. We look for a ___blue___ pond.

2. I _____ we can _____ a map.

3. We can go _____ here.

4. Look! _____ is the pond!

Inflectional Ending -s

TURN and TALK Decode these words with a partner.

taps	naps	claps
dips	sips	tips
gets	lets	pets
hops	mops	stops

MY TURN Write **s** to finish each verb.

Jack ___clap___ his hands.

His dog ___run___ to him.

TURN and TALK Now read the sentences.

Inflectional Ending -s

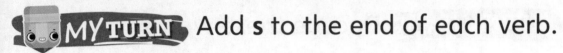 **MY TURN** Add **s** to the end of each verb.

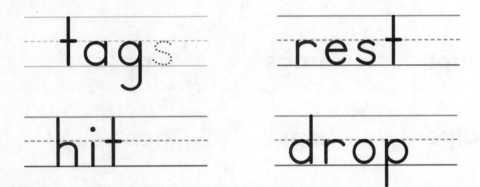

tags   rest

hit   drop

MY TURN Write a sentence using one of the words you wrote.

_____

_____

_____

_____

TURN and TALK Talk with a partner about what each word with inflectional ending **-s** means.

Little Ducks

Duck swims fast from end to end.

She stops at the land.

What do you think is in that nest?

AUDIO

Audio with Highlighting

ANNOTATE

Read the story. Highlight the two words with inflectional ending **-s.**

The nest has eggs!

Duck stops and sits.

She will use the nest
to rest.

Highlight the three words with final
consonant blends.

Look at the little ducks!

One will jump.

The last one gets in the blue pond and swims.

Underline the four words with final consonant blends.

My Learning Goal

I can read informational text.

SPOTLIGHT ON GENRE

Informational Text

Authors write informational text to inform readers about a topic.

TURN and TALK Describe an informational text you have read. What is the author's purpose for writing the text?

Be a Fluent Reader Fluent readers read informational text accurately. That means they read with no mistakes. Remember to take your time and think about the words. Read the words carefully.

Informational Text Anchor Chart

Main Idea

Detail

Detail

Detail

Informational texts inform about a topic.

How Do Baby Animals Grow?

Preview Vocabulary

You will read these words in *How Do Baby Animals Grow?*

| penguin | kangaroo | polar bear |

Read

Read to learn about baby animals.

Look at the pictures to help you understand the topic.

Ask the author a question about the text.

Talk about what you learned from the text.

Meet the Author

Caroline Hutchinson writes books about many science topics, including plants, animals, weather, and the seasons.

How Do Baby Animals Grow?

by Caroline Hutchinson

 AUDIO

Audio with Highlighting

 ANNOTATE

This polar bear makes her home
in the snow. She has her babies
there. They sleep together and
she keeps them warm.

The babies get bigger and bigger.
They play together in the snow.

VOCABULARY IN CONTEXT

What does the word **snow** mean? How does the picture help you figure out what **snow** means?

This kangaroo lives on the grass.
She has a new baby. The baby
lives in her pouch.

The mother gives the baby milk and keeps it warm. The baby gets bigger and bigger.

CLOSE READ

What questions would you ask the author? Highlight the text that you want to ask about.

This penguin makes her home on the ice. The mother penguin lays an egg on the ice.

The baby penguin comes out of the egg. The mother gives the baby food and keeps it warm. The baby gets bigger and bigger.

CLOSE READ

Underline the most important detail the author tells about baby penguins.

Develop Vocabulary

MY TURN <u>Underline</u> the word that names the picture.

kangaroo   penguin

penguin   polar bear

polar bear   penguin

TURN and TALK How can you describe each animal? Respond using the new vocabulary words.

Check for Understanding

MY TURN Write the answers to the questions. You can look back at the text.

1. How can you tell this is an informational text?

_____

_____

_____

_____

2. Why does the author use pictures?

_____

_____

_____

_____

3. Why does a baby animal need its mother? Use text evidence.

_____

_____

_____

_____

_____

Discuss Author's Purpose

Author's purpose is the reason why an author writes a text. Authors write to inform, to entertain, or to persuade.

MY TURN Highlight the author's purpose for writing *How Do Baby Animals Grow?* Look back at the text.

to entertain the reader about baby animals

to inform the reader about baby animals

to persuade the reader to like baby animals

TURN and TALK Talk with a partner about what helped you figure out the author's purpose.

Ask and Answer Questions

Readers generate, or ask, questions to help them understand the author's purpose. They ask questions before, during, and after reading to figure out what the author's purpose might be.

MY TURN Write a question you want to ask the author. Look back at the text.

_____

_____

_____

_____

_____

TURN and TALK Talk with a partner about how the author might answer your questions.

Reflect and Share

Write to Sources

Think about another text you have read this week. On a separate sheet of paper, compare the author's purpose to the author's purpose of *How Do Baby Animals Grow?*

Use Text Evidence

When writing comments about texts, it is important to use examples from the texts. You should:

- Find an example from each text that supports your ideas.
- Explain how the examples support your ideas.

Weekly Question

How are baby animals different from their parents?

I can make and use words to read and write informational text.

Academic Vocabulary

Context clues are words and pictures that can help you learn or clarify the meaning of a word.

MY TURN Read each sentence. Circle the context clue for each underlined word.

1. The class observed the baby animals and <u>noticed</u> how they looked like their parents.

2. The animal's <u>natural</u> home is in the forest.

3. Can you see the way the organized spots make a <u>pattern</u>?

Read Like a Writer, Write for a Reader

Authors organize information in a text to support their reason for writing. The author of this text uses description text structure to organize the topic.

The mother gives the baby food and keeps it warm. The baby gets bigger and bigger. ◄······

The author uses description text structure to explain how the mother helps the baby.

 TURN and TALK Talk about how the author uses description text structure to explain how baby animals grow. Find examples in the text.

MY TURN Using description text structure, write a sentence to explain something to readers.

_____

- -

_____

_____

- -

_____

Spell Words with Final Consonant Blends

Consonant blends are two consonants that are together and spell a blended sound.

MY TURN Write the words in alphabetical order. Look at the first letter. Then look at the second letter.

Spelling Words				My Words to Know
ask	mask	went	pond	use
ramp	held	felt	and	from

1. and

2. _____

3. _____

4. _____

5. _____

6. _____

7. _____

8. _____

9. _____

10. _____

Interrogative Sentences

An **interrogative sentence** asks a question. It begins with a capital letter. It ends with a question mark.

Can you see the duck?
(asks a question)

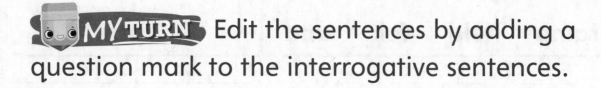 **MY TURN** Edit the sentences by adding a question mark to the interrogative sentences.

1. Is this a pond ___?___

2. Does that duck live here _____

3. Look at the little duck _____

4. Will the duck fly _____

I can write informational text.

Organize with Structure

Authors can organize their writing using a main, or central, idea. They write details that tell about a main idea.

MY TURN Find the main idea and details in an informational book.

Main Idea

_____

_____

_____

Details

_____

_____

_____

MY TURN Develop your informational book by organizing with structure.

Features and Simple Graphics

Authors include features and pictures in their writing to add more details about the text.

MY TURN Write a sentence that supports each picture.

_____

_____

_____

_____

_____

_____

_____

_____

_____

MY TURN Revise your drafts by adding details using features or pictures.

Introduction and Conclusion

An **introduction** is the beginning of the writing. It introduces the topic. A **conclusion** is the ending of the writing.

MY TURN Read the text. <u>Underline</u> the introduction. Write a conclusion sentence.

Baby Penguins

Baby penguins need both parents when they are born. The mother penguin lays the egg. The father penguin keeps the egg warm. When the egg hatches, the mother feeds the baby.

MY TURN Develop an introduction and conclusion for your informational book.

Changing with the Seasons

 **MY TURN** (Circle) the name of each season.

Spring

A **snowshoe hare** has brown fur.

A **little brown bat** wakes up from hibernation.

Summer

How do animals change with the seasons?

Fall

A **snowshoe hare** has white fur.

A **little brown bat** starts its hibernation.

Winter

Rhyming Words

SEE and SAY Rhyming words have the same middle and ending sounds. Say each picture name. Produce, or say, other words that rhyme with the picture names.

Consonant Digraphs sh, th

The letters **sh** make the sound at the beginning of **ship** or at the end of **wish**.

The letters **th** make the sound at the beginning of **thick,** at the beginning of **the**, or at the end of **path.**

MY TURN Read each word.

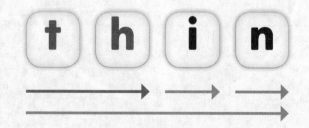

Consonant Digraphs sh, th

TURN and TALK Decode these words with a partner.

bath	math	path
dish	fish	wish
that	them	then
shed	shell	shelf

MY TURN Write **sh** or **th** to finish the words.

1. Jon walks to a _____ op _____ .

2. He is _____ wi _____ his mom.

TURN and TALK Now read the sentences.

Consonant Digraphs sh, th

MY TURN Read the picture names. <u>Underline</u> the digraph in each picture name.

fi<u>sh</u>   bath   shell

MY TURN Write a sentence that includes a word with **sh** or **th**.

_____

- -

_____

- -

_____

- -

_____

Rhyming Words

SEE and SAY Rhyming words have the same middle and ending sounds. Say each picture name. Say a series, or list, of rhyming words.

Inflectional Ending -ing

The ending **-ing** on a verb shows that someone or something is, was, or will be doing something.

MY TURN Read the sentences.

One cat is miss**ing.**

Two cats are miss**ing.**

We are look**ing** for the cats!

My Words to Know

Some words you must remember and practice.

MY TURN Read the words.

all	too	her	goes	make

MY TURN Write words from the box to complete the sentences. Read the sentences.

1. Kim has _all_ the hats by _____.

2. She _____ to the shop for hats.

3. Do you like hats _____ ?

4. We can _____ a hat hut!

Inflectional Ending -ing

TURN and TALK Read these words with a partner.

telling	yelling	selling

kicking	licking	ticking

MY TURN What is the person doing in each picture? Write **-ing** to finish each word.

plant<u>ing</u>   brush

TURN and TALK Now read the words. What do the words mean?

Inflectional Ending -ing

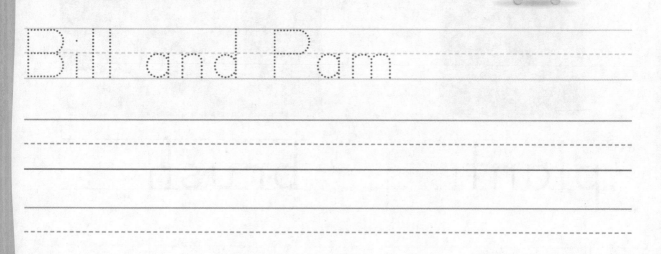 **MY TURN** Read the sentences. <u>Underline</u> the words that tell what Bill and Pam are doing.

Bill and Pam are <u>packing</u> a bag.

Bill is looking for his sock.

Pam is helping Bill.

> Words with the ending **-ing** often come after the word **is** or **are**.

MY TURN Write another sentence about Bill and Pam that tells something they are doing.

Bill and Pam

Beth and Nash

Beth has to rush to the path.

She goes to get nuts.

All the nuts make Beth glad.

AUDIO

Audio with Highlighting

ANNOTATE

Read the story. Highlight the four words with the same ending sound as **bath.**

131

Nash is <u>helping</u> Beth too.

They are fixing her den.

They will go from thin
to thick.

<u>Underline</u> the two words with the
inflectional ending **-ing.**

Beth and Nash are resting.

They have the nuts on a dish.

The nuts are fresh. Yum!

Highlight the three words
with the **sh** sound.

Read Together

My Learning Goal

I can read about how living things grow and change.

Poetry

Poetry is written in lines. It can have rhyme, or words with the same middle and ending sounds. It often has rhythm, or a strong beat.

Rhythm ─ Hickory, dickory, dock,

The mouse ran up the clock;

Rhyme The clock struck one,

And down he run,

Hickory, dickory, dock.

TURN and TALK How is poetry different from informational text?

Poetry Anchor Chart

Rhyme

cat rhymes with **rat**

Rhythm

The mŏŭse ran ŭp the clŏck
ta DUM   ta DUM   ta DUM

Poetry Collection

Preview Vocabulary

You will read these words in the poems this week.

eat	dig	sleep	burrow

Read

Read to understand rhythm and rhyme.

Look at the illustrations to help you understand the poems.

Ask questions during reading to better understand the poems.

Talk about what you find interesting.

Meet *the* Author

Chitra Banerjee Divakaruni was born in India. Many of her books talk about what it's like to come live in America.

Poetry Collection

The Long Sleep

Changes

written by Chitra Divakaruni
illustrated by Ian Joven

 AUDIO

Audio with Highlighting

 ANNOTATE

The Long Sleep

written by Chitra Divakaruni
illustrated by Ian Joven

When red leaves fall,

I eat all day.

Then dig my den—
No time to play.

CLOSE READ

Read the pages aloud. Clap the beat of the poem. <u>Underline</u> the words you clapped on.

Full and happy,
I sleep and sleep
Through winter's chill
And snowfalls deep.

CLOSE READ

Highlight the words that tell how the bear changes when winter comes.

Changes

written by Chitra Divakaruni
illustrated by Ian Joven

In spring and summer

My coat is brown.

I blend with dirt.

I burrow down.

CLOSE READ

<u>Underline</u> the lines that rhyme.

In icy winter

My coat turns white.

It's hard to find me,

Day or night.

CLOSE READ

Highlight the words that tell how the fox changes with the seasons.

Develop Vocabulary

MY TURN Write the word that finishes each sentence.

eat	dig	sleep	burrow

Foxes <u>burrow</u> into the dirt.

Bears _____ their own dens.

They _____ through the winter.

Bears _____ lots of food before winter.

TURN and TALK Talk with your partner about how the words in the box are alike.

Check for Understanding

MY TURN Write the answers to the questions. You can look back at the text.

1. What makes these texts poetry?

_____

_____

_____

2. Why does the author use the words **chill** and **icy?**

_____

_____

_____

3. How is the bear like the fox? Use text evidence.

_____

_____
_____

_____

Describe Elements of Poetry

Poems can have rhyme and rhythm. Words that **rhyme** have the same middle and ending sounds. **Rhythm** is a regular pattern of beats.

MY TURN Draw a picture that shows the lines that rhyme in "Changes." Look back at the text.

TURN and TALK Clap the rhythm of "The Long Sleep" with a partner. Look back at the text.

Create New Understandings

You make new understandings when you synthesize, or put together, information as you read.

MY TURN What new understanding can you make with these details? Look back at the texts.

Details	Details

My New Understanding

_____

_____

_____

_____

_____

Reflect and Share

Talk About It

You read about how a fox and a bear change with the seasons. What other animals have you learned about that change in some way? How are those animals like the fox or bear?

Listening to Others

When talking with others, it is important to:

- Listen politely.

- Look at the person who is speaking.

Use the words on the note to help you.

Now share your ideas.

> What do you think. . .?
> I think . . .

Weekly Question

How do animals change with the seasons?

I can make and use words to connect reading and writing.

Academic Vocabulary

Word parts are added to some words to make new words with different meanings.

The word part **-less** means "**without**."

The word part **un-** means "**not**."

MY TURN Write the correct word part to make a word that fits the definition.

	Definition
pattern|ess	without a pattern
noticed	not noticed
sense	without sense

Read Like a Writer, Write for a Reader

Authors use words to help readers imagine the way things look, feel, sound, taste, and smell.

Through **winter's** chill ◄······· And snowfall deep

The author chose this word to help readers visualize winter.

TURN and TALK How does the word **chill** help you visualize, or imagine, winter?

MY TURN Write sentences with words that tell how your classroom looks, sounds, or smells. The words should help you visualize the classroom.

_____

- -

_____

- -

_____

- -

_____

I can write informational text.

Edit for Capitalization

Authors capitalize the beginning of sentences, the word **I**, the days, the months, and the names of people.

Sam and **I** will meet on a **F**riday in **M**ay.

MY TURN Edit the capital letters in these sentences. Write the correct words.

1. what day in june is jon coming?

_____

_____

2. he and i are coming on monday.

_____

_____

3. can i bring my dog?

_____

_____

MY TURN Edit for capital letters in your informational book.

Edit for Nouns

A **possessive noun** tells who or what owns something.

the fox's fur (**apostrophe s** shows that one fox owns the fur)

the bears' den (apostrophe after the **s** shows that two or more bears own the den)

MY TURN Name the animals in the pictures. Then write about what the animals own.

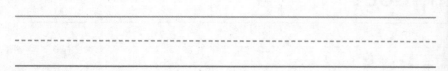

cat's yarn

MY TURN Edit for nouns in your informational book.

Edit for Complete Sentences with Subject-Verb Agreement

A sentence tells a complete idea. It has a subject and a verb that must match.

Add **-s** to verbs that tell what one subject is doing now.

Do not add **-s** to verbs that tell what two or more subjects are doing now.

MY TURN Edit the underlined subject and verb in these sentences.

1. The <u>bear sleep</u> in the winter.

   bear sleeps

2. <u>Arctic foxes digs</u> in the dirt.

MY TURN Edit your informational book for subject-verb agreement.

Growing Older

When I turned one,
I learned how to walk.
The world was so new
when I started to talk.

When I was three,
I slid down and climbed up.
I could put on my shoes;
I could drink from a cup.

How do people grow and change?

Now I am six.
I can run and play ball.
I'm learning new things
even though I seem small.

Soon I'll be eight!
I can't wait to see
how big and how smart
I will grow up to be.

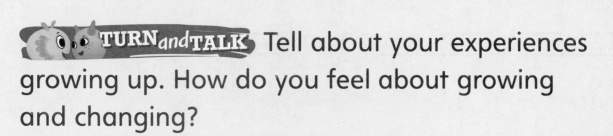 **TURN and TALK** Tell about your experiences growing up. How do you feel about growing and changing?

Change Sounds

 **SEE and SAY** Say each picture name. Then change the beginning sound. Say the new word.

Long a Spelled VCe

The vowel-consonant-e pattern (VCe) makes vowels long. A long vowel says its name.
The letter **a** can make the long **a** sound you hear in **tape**.

MY TURN Read these words.

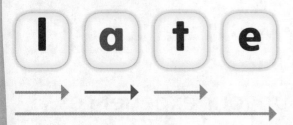

Long a Spelled VCe

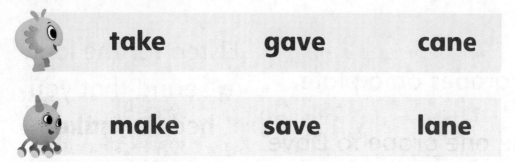 **TURN and TALK** Decode these words with a partner.

take	**gave**	**cane**
make	**save**	**lane**

MY TURN Say each picture name. Write **a** to finish each word. Match each picture to the word that names it.

l a k e

p l _ te

gr _ pe

Long a Spelled VCe

MY TURN Read the sentences. Highlight words with the long **a** sound.

Kate ate grapes on a plate.

Kate gave one grape to Dave.

Can she bake a cake too?

Listen for the long **a** sound that you hear in **make.**

MY TURN Write a sentence using words with long **a** spelled **a_e.**

_____

_____

_____

Middle Sounds

SEE and SAY Say each sound as you name each picture. Listen to the middle sound. Then say the picture names again.

Vowel Sound in ball

The letters **a**, **al**, and **aw** can spell the vowel sound you hear in **ball**.

MY TURN Read these words.

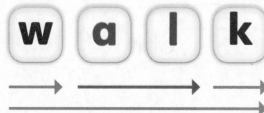

c a l l   p a w

w a l k

My Words to Know

Some words you must remember and practice.

MY TURN Read these words.

four	five	ride	part	your

MY TURN Use words from the box to complete the sentences. Then read the sentences.

1. Jane is _four_ or _____.

2. She can _____ fast.

3. Can she go to _____ game?

4. She will see _____ of it.

Vowel Sound in ball

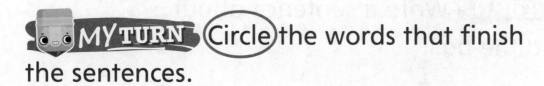 **TURN and TALK** Read these words with a partner.

lawn	**yawn**	**crawl**
small	**wall**	**mall**
talk	**chalk**	**walk**
paw	**saw**	**draw**

MY TURN (Circle) the words that finish the sentences.

1. Dave (saw / sat) Kate.

2. They will (take / talk).

3. Then they will go to the (mall / map).

Vowel Sound in ball

MY TURN Read the sentences. <u>Underline</u> the words that have the same vowel sound as **ball**.

Jake is <u>small</u>.

He can not talk well.

He sees a ball.

He will walk to get it.

> The letters **al** and **aw** spell the vowel sound you hear in **ball.**

MY TURN Write a sentence about Jake and the ball.

_____

_____

_____

_____

Brave Jane

Jane is a small kid.

She is not four. She is five.

She can walk her dog.

She can draw one part.

AUDIO

Audio with Highlighting

ANNOTATE

Read the story. Highlight the three words with the same vowel sound as **ball.**

Can Jane ride?

Mom came to help.

Jane goes fast.

Use your brakes, Jane!

Underline the five words with long **a**.

Jane waves to Mom from the gate.

She stands tall.

Brave Jane can ride!

Highlight the five words with long **a.**

Drama

A drama, or play, is a story that is written to be acted out for others. It has characters and a setting. It has dialogue, or what the characters say.

Setting → **In the living room**

Characters → Kim: It's snowing! I need my coat.

Dad: It is too small.

Dialogue → Wear this bigger one.

Kim: Thanks, Dad.

TURN and TALK How is a play different from informational text?

Drama Anchor Chart

Drama has...

Characters
the people in the drama

Setting
when and where the story takes place

Plot
the story

Dialogue
words the characters say

Bigger Shoes for the Big Race

Preview Vocabulary

You will read these words in *Bigger Shoes for the Big Race*.

big	new	fast	small

Read

Look at the pictures. Make a prediction, or guess, about the text.

Read to check if your prediction is correct.

Ask questions about confusing parts.

Talk about the events with a partner.

Meet the Author

Wade Hudson writes to tell about the lives of African Americans. Wade thinks good books make a difference in children's lives.

Bigger Shoes for the Big Race

written by Wade Hudson
illustrated by Tracy Bishop

Characters
TIMMY CALVIN DARIUS

Setting
LIVING ROOM

 AUDIO

Audio with Highlighting

 ANNOTATE

TIMMY: Look at my fast running shoes. They are too small.

DARIUS: Look at my superfast running shoes. They are too small too.

CLOSE READ

A drama, or play, has characters.
Underline the names of the characters.

TIMMY: I need new running shoes. I have a big race.

DARIUS: I need new running shoes. I have a big race too.

CLOSE READ

Highlight the details that help you know about the characters. Use the picture too.

Timmy points to Darius's shoes.

TIMMY: Can I have your superfast running shoes, Darius?

DARIUS: You can have my superfast running shoes, Timmy.

CLOSE READ

Drama has dialogue that tells what the characters say. <u>Underline</u> the dialogue.

DARIUS: But now I don't have any superfast running shoes. What should I do?

TIMMY: Maybe Calvin can help.

Calvin enters, smiling.

CALVIN: My superfast running shoes are too small for me. You can have them, Darius.

TIMMY AND DARIUS: Now we both have shoes for the big race!

CLOSE READ

Highlight the details that help you know about the characters. Use the pictures too.

Develop Vocabulary

Words may have the same general meaning but still have slightly different meanings, or **shades of meaning.**

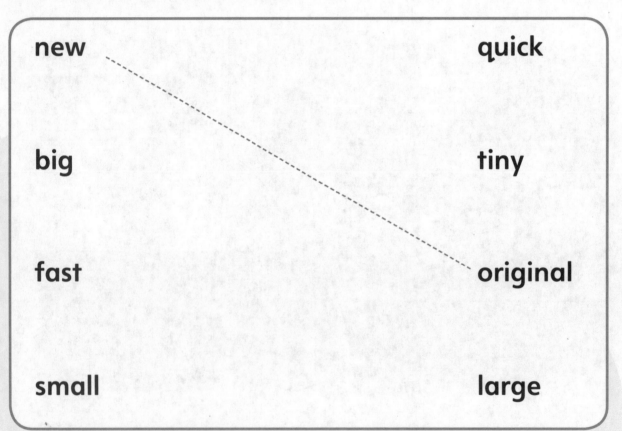

MY TURN Match the words that have the same general meaning.

new	**quick**
big	**tiny**
fast	**original**
small	**large**

TURN and TALK Find the word pairs in a dictionary. Discuss how the words in each pair have slightly different meanings.

Check for Understanding

MY TURN Write the answers to the questions. You can look back at the text.

1. What parts of the text help you know that it is a drama, or play?

_____

- -

_____

- -

_____

2. What does the author want us to think about as we read this text?

_____

- -

_____

- -

_____

3. Why is Calvin able to help? Use text evidence.

_____

- -

_____

- -

_____

Find Elements of Drama

A drama, or play, has characters, a setting, and dialogue. **Dialogue** is the words the characters say.

MY TURN What elements of a play are in *Bigger Shoes for the Big Race?* Look back at the text.

Characters

Setting

Dialogue

TURN and TALK Talk about the characters and setting in the play *Bigger Shoes for the Big Race.*

Make Inferences

Readers make inferences when they use what they know and what they read to figure out the text.

MY TURN What inference can you make about the characters? Look back at the text.

Timmy and Darius like to _____

_____

_____

Calvin is _____

_____

because _____

_____

_____

_____

TURN and TALK Talk about the text evidence that supports your inference.

Reflect and Share

Write to Sources

Think about the texts you have read this week. Which text did you like best? On a separate sheet of paper, write your opinion.

State an Opinion

When you state your opinion, you tell what you think or feel about a topic. You should:

- Tell a reason for your opinion.
- Use the word **because** to tell your reason.
- Use examples from the text to support your opinion.

Weekly Question

How do people grow and change?

Read Together

I can make and use words to connect reading and writing.

My Learning Goal

Academic Vocabulary

MY TURN Read each sentence. Mark **yes** or **no**.

	Yes	No
It's **natural** for living things to grow and change.		
Flowers can have **patterns.**		
Our five senses help us **notice** things.		
It's important to have a **reason** to support an opinion.		

TURN and TALK Talk about your answers with a partner. Respond using new vocabulary words.

187

Read Like a Writer, Write for a Reader

Sometimes authors choose interesting words to describe something that is important.

Look at my **superfast running shoes.**

◄········· The author uses an interesting adjective to describe the shoes.

 MY TURN Write about something that is important to you. Use an interesting word to describe it.

_____

_____

_____

_____

_____

_____

Spell Long a Words

Long **a** words can be spelled **a_e.**

 **MY TURN** Sort and spell the words.

Spelling Words			
came	cake	take	name
make	bake	same	shake

-ake

make

-ame

My Words to Know

four   your

MY TURN Find three spelling words in a dictionary.

189

Imperative Sentences

An **imperative sentence** gives a command or makes a request. It begins with a capital letter and ends with a period.

Take out a pencil. (gives a command)
Look at me, please. (makes a request)

MY TURN Edit the punctuation marks for these imperative sentences.

1. Give me the shoes? _____

2. Max, turn the page! _____

3. Look to the left? _____

MY TURN Write an imperative sentence.

_____

_____

_____

I can write informational text.

Edit for Capitalization

Review the rules for capitalization.

Use a capital letter:
- at the beginnings of sentences
- for the word **I**
- for the names of people
- for months and days in dates

MY TURN Underline the words that need a capital letter.

On <u>may</u> 12, i went to the zoo. My sister jess wanted to see the new giraffe. we watched the baby giraffe play with its mom.

MY TURN Edit for capitalization in your informational book.

Edit for Commas

A comma is used in dates. Commas are used to separate the words in a list, or series.

June 10, 2020 (comma between the date and year)

We can run, swim, and jump. (comma after each word in a list)

MY TURN Add commas to the correct place in each sentence.

1. The race is on May 17, 2020.

2. We need shoes shorts and hats.

3. Let's celebrate the race on June 2 2020.

4. Can you bring chalk tape and a horn?

MY TURN Edit your informational book for commas.

Assessment

In this unit, you have learned how to write an informational book.

MY TURN Read the list. Put a check next to what you can do.

☐ I can brainstorm a topic and a main idea.

☐ I can organize my informational book.

☐ I can write an introduction and a conclusion.

☐ I can add facts and details.

☐ I can make pictures.

☐ I can use correct nouns and verbs.

☐ I can edit for capital letters and commas.

COMPARE ACROSS TEXTS

UNIT THEME

I Spy

 MY TURN

Look back at each text.
Find a picture that
shows how a living thing
grows and changes.
Write the page number
of the picture.

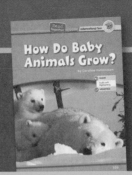

How Do Baby Animals Grow?

Example of change:

Page _____

WEEK 3

BOOK CLUB

WEEK 2

The Life Cycle of a Sunflower

Example of change:

Page _____

BOOK CLUB

WEEK 1

The Life of a Frog

Example of change:

Page _____

**"The Long Sleep"
"Changes"**

Example of change:

Page _____ _____ _____

WEEK
4

WEEK
5

**Bigger Shoes
for the Big Race**

Example of change:

Page _____ _____ _____

Essential Question

MY TURN

How do living things grow
and change?

WEEK
6

Project

Now it's time to apply what
you learned about growing
and changing in your **WEEK 6
PROJECT: New at the Zoo!**

Change Sounds

 **SEE and SAY** Say the name of each picture. Then change the beginning sound. Say the new word.

Long i Spelled VCe

In words spelled vowel-consonant-**e**, the letter **i** spells the long **i** sound you hear in **bike**. The **e** is silent.

MY TURN Read these words.

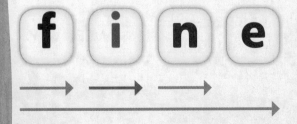

l i f e

f i n e

Long i Spelled VCe

 TURN and TALK Decode these words.

| dine | mine | line |

| kite | bite | quite |

| like | hike | spike |

| hide | wide | ride |

MY TURN Write **i** to finish each word.

b i ke

sl i de

d i me

l i me

197

Long i Spelled VCe

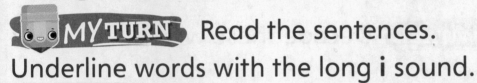 **MY TURN** Read the sentences.
Underline words with the long **i** sound.

<u>Mike</u> goes on the slide.

The slide is fine.

Do you like to slide?

Mike will slide one time.

> Listen for the long **i** sound you hear in **ride**.

MY TURN Write a new
sentence about the slide.

_____

- -

_____

_____

- -

_____

Spell Long i Words

Long **i** words can be spelled **i_e**.

 Sort and spell the words.

Spelling Words			
hide	fine	side	dine
bike	like	ride	hike

-ine

fine

-ide

-ike

My Words to Know
don't   know

Different Sounds

 **SEE and SAY** You can listen for sounds that are alike and different. Say the name of each picture. Listen to the middle sound. Tell which picture name has the short **i** sound. Tell which picture name has the long **i** sound.

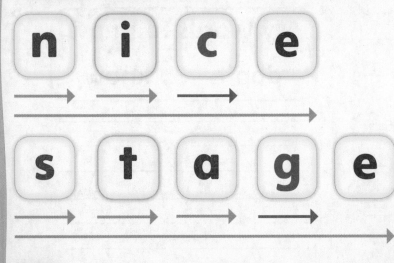

s Sound Spelled c; j Sound Spelled g

Sometimes the letter **c** can make the **s** sound like you hear in **mice**. Sometimes the letter **g** can make the **j** sound like you hear in **cage**.

MY TURN Read these words.

n i c e

s t a g e

s Sound Spelled c
j Sound Spelled g

MY TURN Read the sentences.
Underline words with the **s** sound spelled **c.**
Highlight words with the **j** sound spelled **g.**

The little <u>mice</u> are on stage.

They are not in a cage.

There is a smile on my face.

The mice had a race.

MY TURN Write a sentence about the mice.

The mice

Too Many Pups!

 AUDIO

Audio with
Highlighting

ANNOTATE

Mike is my <u>age</u>.

He has too many pups.

They are nice.

They don't bite. But they run!

I know they will get big.

<u>Underline</u> the words with the **s** sound spelled **c** and the **j** sound spelled **g.**

Grace likes this pup.

Max likes this pup.

It is time to go.

Highlight the words that have long **i** spelled VCe.

Mike went back into the den.

After two pups go, just one is left.

Mike smiles.

One pup is not too many!

Highlight the words that have long **i** spelled VCe.

New at the ZOO!

Activity

Your local zoo wants to add a new animal. Write a letter to the zookeeper. Tell your opinion about which animal it should be and why.

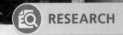 **RESEARCH**

Let's Read!

This week you will read three articles about animals.

1. Animals in Zoos
2. Schools Need Bird-Watching Clubs
3. Safari Adventure

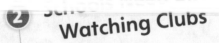 **COLLABORATE** With a partner, choose an animal to research. What are two questions you have about this animal?

Use Academic Words

COLLABORATE You learned many new academic words in this unit. With your partner, use some of these new words to talk about the picture.

Zoo Animal Research Plan

Day 1 Generate questions for research.

Day 2 Research an animal.

Day 3 Write a letter to the zookeeper.

Day 4 Revise and edit the letter.

Day 5 Present the letter to classmates.

What Do You Think?

Sometimes authors try to get you to think or do something. Think about the reasons an author gives. Use what you learn to write your letter.

COLLABORATE With a partner, read "Schools Need Bird-Watching Clubs." Then fill in the chart about the article.

Author's Opinion	
What does the author want you to think?	
Author's Reasons	
What reasons does the author give?	
Persuasive Words	
Can you find any persuasive words?	

Ask an Expert!

🔍 RESEARCH

A **source** is a person, book, or Web site that has information to help answer questions.

My zoo animal is _____.

Two questions about my animal are

_____

_____

_____

_____

_____

COLLABORATE (Circle) the source where you will look for information to answer your questions.

books   **computer**   **librarian**

Opinion Letter

Opinion letters include opinions, reasons, facts, and persuasive words to try to convince readers to think or do something.

Dear Zookeeper Hernandez,

Persuasive Word

I think polar bears are the **Opinion**

best animal to add to the zoo.

People will be happy to watch **Reason**

them grow up. Polar bears are

small when they are born. **Fact**

But they get big quickly!

From,

Susan Gavin and

Dianne Laux

Read Together

Go to the Zoo!

RESEARCH

COLLABORATE If you need more information to answer your questions, you can try a zoo Web site. Follow these steps:

1. Go to your favorite zoo Web site.

2. Enter your animal name in the search window.

3. Find a new fact about your animal.

COLLABORATE With a partner, find a new fact about your animal.

My new fact: _____

Take a Picture!

You can make your letter stronger by adding a picture or diagram.

Photographs and drawings help your readers picture your topic.

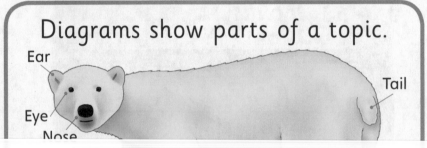

Diagrams show parts of a topic.

Ear

Tail

Eye

Nose

Claws

Foot

 **COLLABORATE** With a partner, choose a drawing, photo, or diagram to show the class when you present your project.

Revise

 COLLABORATE Read your letter to your partner.

Did you check your

opinion?	yes	no
reasons?	yes	no
facts?	yes	no

Did you circle **yes** or **no**?

Edit

 COLLABORATE Read your letter again.

Check for

☐ spelling

☐ punctuation

☐ capital letters

Share

 **COLLABORATE** Present, or share, your letter.

Remember to follow the rules for **speaking and listening.**

- Speak clearly at an appropriate pace.
- Follow the conventions of language.
- Listen actively.

Reflect

MY TURN Complete the sentences.

One thing I like about my letter is

_____

_____

_____

Something I would change next time is

_____

_____

_____

_____

Reflect on Your Goals

Look back at your unit goals. Use a different color to rate yourself again.

MY TURN Complete the sentences.

Reflect on Your Reading

My favorite text I read on my own is

Reflect on Writing

My best writing from this unit is

How to Use a Picture Dictionary

You can use a picture dictionary to find words. The words are grouped into topics. The topic of this picture dictionary is **directions** and **positions**. Look at the pictures, and try to read the words. The pictures will help you understand the meanings of the words.

This is the word you are learning.

This is a picture of the word.

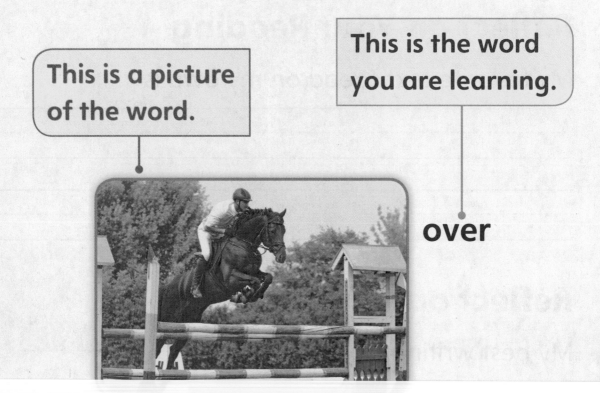

over

TURNand**TALK** Find the word **under** in the picture dictionary. To be sure you understand what the word means, use the word in a few sentences.

Directions and Positions

up

down

under

top

bottom

front

back

How to Use a Digital Resource

An online dictionary, or **digital resource**, can help you find the meanings of words that are not in this glossary. Type the word you are looking for in the search box. When you hit return, the word and meaning will pop up.

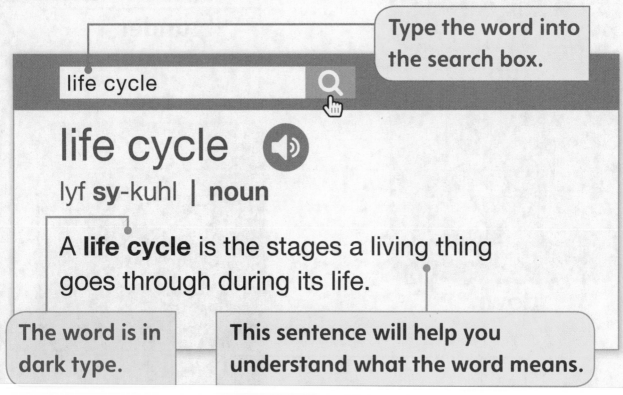

Type the word into the search box.

life cycle

life cycle 🔊

lyf **sy**-kuhl | **noun**

A **life cycle** is the stages a living thing goes through during its life.

The word is in dark type.

This sentence will help you understand what the word means.

MY TURN Find the word **hibernate** using a digital resource. Draw a picture of what the word means.

Bb

big **Big** is another word for large.

buds **Buds** are partly opened flowers.

burrow When animals **burrow**, they dig a hole in the ground to hide themselves.

Dd

dig When animals **dig**, they use their claws to make a hole in the ground.

Ee

eat When people or animals **eat**, they chew and swallow food.

eggs • kangaroo

eggs Eggs are round or oval objects from which young animals are hatched.

Ff

fast Fast means quick.

frog A **frog** is a small animal with smooth skin, webbed feet, and long back legs for jumping.

Gg

gills Gills are a body part that helps fish and tadpoles breathe underwater.

Kk

kangaroo A **kangaroo** is an Australian animal that has small front legs and very strong back legs for jumping. A female has a pouch in front to carry a baby.

Ll

leaves **Leaves** are the flat green parts of a plant.

Nn

nature **Nature** is everything in the world not made by people.

new When something is **new**, it is not old. It is not used yet.

notice When you **notice** something, you see it or observe it.

Pp

pattern A **pattern** is a design. It is the way colors or shapes appear over and over again in order.

penguin • small

penguin A **penguin** is a sea bird that dives and swims with flippers but does not fly.

polar bear A **polar bear** is a large white bear that lives in the Arctic.

Rr

reason A **reason** is whatever explains why something happened.

Ss

sleep When you **sleep**, you rest your body and mind.

small Small means not large in size, amount, or number.

224

soil **Soil** is the top layer of the earth or dirt.

stems **Stems** are the main supporting part of a plant above the ground.

Tt

tadpole A **tadpole** is a creature that becomes a frog.

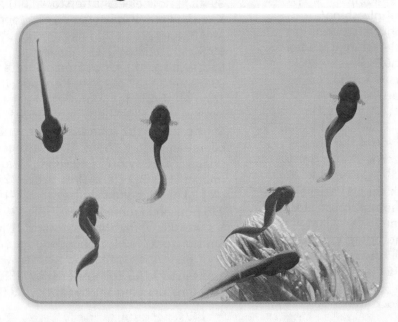